KB185848

나만의 멋진

영어
필기체 완성

나만의 멋진
영어 필기체 완성

초판 1쇄 인쇄 2016년 8월 31일
초판 1쇄 발행 2016년 9월 9일
2판 1쇄 발행 2025년 2월 6일

지은이	글꼴연구소
발행인	임충배
홍보/마케팅	양경자
편집	김인숙, 왕혜영
디자인	이경자, 김혜원
펴낸곳	마들렌 북
제작	(주)피앤엠123

출판신고 2014년 4월 3일
등록번호 제406-2014-000035호

경기도 파주시 산남로 183-25
TEL 031-946-3196 / FAX 050-4244-9979
홈페이지 www.pub365.co.kr

ISBN 979-11-94543-01-5 13740
© 2025 PUB.365

· 저자와 출판사의 허락 없이 내용 일부를 인용하거나 발췌하는 것을 금합니다.
· 저자와의 협의에 의하여 인지는 붙이지 않습니다.
· 가격은 뒤표지에 있습니다.
· 잘못 만들어진 책은 구입처에서 바꾸어 드립니다.

나만의 멋진

영어 필기체 완성

저자 글꼴연구소

Cursive Handwriting

Mædəlin Buk

How to

① Before & After
첫 장의 필기체 연습 이전 글자와 맨 마지막 장의 필기체 연습 이후의 차이를 비교해보세요. 달라진 나의 모습을 찾을 수 있습니다.

② 선 연습
지금까지 우리는 컴퓨터 자판 두드리는 것에 너무 익숙해 있습니다. 손으로 글을 쓰기 위한 첫 단계입니다. 직접 글을 쓰기 위해 손부터 풀어줘야 할 것 같네요. 준비되셨죠? 자~ 지금부터 시작입니다.

③ 알파벳 쓰기
A~Z, a~z까지 필기체를 쓰기 위해 기초적인 알파벳 연습을 진행합니다. 처음에는 누구나 글자를 쓰는 것이 아닌 그림을 그리고 있네요. 끝까지 연습해보세요.

④ 테마별 단어 연습
우리나라 및 외국의 남자/여자 이름, 숫자/월/요일, 생일 등 기념일 등 기본적인 단어를 연습합니다.

⑤ 자주 쓰는 패턴 연습
자주 쓰는 접두사/접미사, 일상 회화에서 많이 쓰이는 패턴의 평서형/의문형을 집중적으로 연습합니다. 자주 나오는 글이만큼 더욱 자연스럽게 쓰도록 연습하세요.

⑥ 단문 / 장문 연습
삶에 본보기가 되는 짧은 명언부터 나만의 일기, 상대방과 소통을 위한 편지 등의 장문 따라 쓰기까지 순차적으로 연습하여 마무리합니다.

Contents

* 홈페이지(www.pub365.co.kr)에서 필기체 연습용 워크시트를 다운받을 수 있습니다.

나만의 멋진 영어 필기체 만들기 첫 시작입니다.

아래 문장을 그려보세요.

The real effort never betrays me!

The real effort never betrays me!
진정한 노력은 결코 나를 배신하지 않는다!

❶

❷

❸

Part 1

기본 연습

홈페이지(www.pub365.co.kr)에서 필기체 연습용 워크시트를 다운받을 수 있습니다.

A	B	C	D
E	F	G	H
I	J	K	L
M	N	O	P
Q	R	S	T
U	V	W	X
Y	Z		

홈페이지(www.pub365.co.kr)에서 필기체 연습용 워크시트를 다운받을 수 있습니다.

a	b	c	d
a	b	c	d

e	f	g	h
e	f	g	h

i	j	k	l
2. 1 i	2. 1 j	k	l

m	n	o	p
m	n	o	p

q	r	s	t
q	r	s	2 1 t

u	v	w	x
u	v	w	1 x 2

y	z		
y	z		

손풀기 연습을 해볼까요? 아래 모양대로 따라 그려보세요.

α α α α α α α

β β β β β β β

γ γ γ γ γ γ

δ δ δ δ δ δ δ

ε ε ε ε ε ε

ζ ζ ζ ζ ζ ζ

σ σ σ σ σ σ σ

τ τ τ τ τ τ τ

υ υ υ υ υ υ υ

φ φ φ φ φ φ

ψ ψ ψ ψ ψ ψ

ω ω ω ω ω ω ω

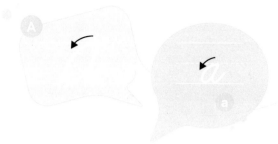

Tip

대문자 A와 소문자 a는 크기만 다르고 모양은 동일합니다.
하지만 대문자는 이렇게 $\mathcal{A}$ 쓰기도 합니다.

a a a a a a a a

a a a a a a a a

act
행동하다

act   *act act act*

about
～에 관하여

about   *about about about*

airport
공항

airport   *airport airport airport*

around
주변에, ～경에

around   *around around around*

대문자 B와 소문자 b는 모양이 많이 다르네요. 줄에 맞춰
천천히 따라 써보세요.

B B B B B B B

b b b b b b b

big
큰
big　　*big big big*

ball
공
ball　　*ball ball ball*

book
책
book　　*book book book*

because
왜냐하면
because　　*because because because*

13

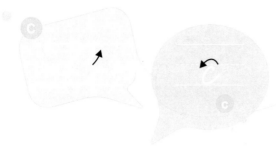

Tip

대문자 C와 소문자 c는 크기만 다르고 모양은 동일합니다.
하지만 대문자는 $\mathscr{C}$ 로 쓰기도 합니다.

C C C C C C C

c c c c c c c

car
차

car   car car car

city
도시

city   city city city

corner
모퉁이

corner   corner corner corner

curtain
커튼

curtain   curtain curtain curtain

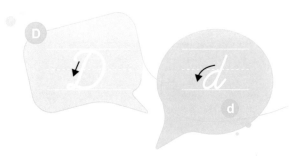

Tip

어렵지 않게 따라 쓸 수 있습니다. 소문자 d 마지막에 굽어
올려지는 부분이 다른 글자와 이어집니다.

D D D D D D D D D

d d d d d d

day
날, 낮

day   *day day day*

dish
접시

dish   *dish dish dish*

dream
꿈

dream   *dream dream dream*

danger
위험

danger   *danger danger danger*

15

Tip
대문자 E의 윗부분은 작게, 아래는 좀 크게 쓰세요. 소문자 e는 아랫부분이 위 둥근 부분을 감싸듯 약간 크게 씁니다.

$\mathcal{E}$ $\mathcal{E}$ $\mathcal{E}$ $\mathcal{E}$ $\mathcal{E}$ $\mathcal{E}$ $\mathcal{E}$ $\mathcal{E}$

e e e e e e e

eat
먹다

eat   *eat eat eat*

egg
알

egg   *egg egg egg*

excite
흥분시키다

excite   *excite excite excite*

example
예, 보기

example   *example example example*

대문자 F는 3획으로 씁니다. 하지만 1~2번을 한 획으로 쓸
수 있으니 연습하시면서 본인의 스타일을 완성하세요.

$\mathcal{F}$ $\mathcal{F}$ $\mathcal{F}$ $\mathcal{F}$ $\mathcal{F}$ $\mathcal{F}$ $\mathcal{F}$

f f f f f f f

fat
뚱뚱한

fat

fat fat fat

fish
물고기

fish

fish fish fish

from
~로 부터

from

from from from

family
가족

family

family family family

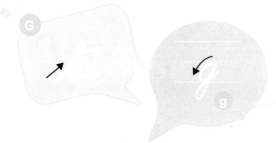

Tip

대문자 G는 우리가 알고 있는 기본 알파벳의 모양과 많이 다릅니다. 눈에 익숙해지도록 많이 보고 연습하세요.

G G G G G G

g g g g g g

gas
가스

gas   *gas gas gas*

grow
자라다, 키우다

grow   *grow grow grow*

give
주다

give   *give give give*

ground
운동장, 땅

ground   *ground ground ground*

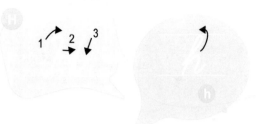

Tip

대문자 H는 3획으로 씁니다. 하지만 1~3번을 이어서 한 획
으로 쓸 수 있으니 연습해보세요.

H H H H H H H H

h h h h h h h h

hot
더운, 뜨거운

hot   *hot hot hot*

how
어떻게

how   *how how how*

hello
안녕

hello   *hello hello hello*

happy
행복한

happy   *happy happy happy*

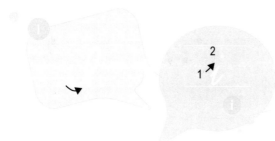

Tip

소문자 i / j / t / x 는 한 획으로 이어 쓸 수 없습니다.
점과 선은 맨 마지막에 쓰세요.

l l l l l l

i i i i i i i

if
만약 ~한다면

if   *if if if*

ink
잉크

ink   *ink ink ink*

idea
생각, 아이디어

idea   *idea idea idea*

island
섬

island   *island island island*

대문자 J는 소문자 g (g)와 비슷합니다. 윗부분의 크기와
모양이 조금 다름을 확인하세요.

g g g g g g

j j j j j j

job
일

job

job job job

just
단지

just

just just just

jump
뛰다

jump

jump jump jump

jungle
정글

jungle

jungle jungle jungle

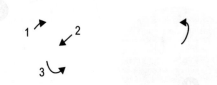

Tip

대문자 K는 3획으로 씁니다. 하지만 2~3번을 한 획으로 쓸 수 있으니 연습하면서 자신의 스타일을 완성하세요.

K K K K K K K

k k k k k k k

key
열쇠

key

key key key

king
왕

king

king king king

know
알다

know

know know know

kitchen
부엌

kitchen

kitchen kitchen kitchen

22

소문자는 왼쪽 아래부터 쓰게 됩니다. 시작 부분이 오른쪽
끝부분의 위치와 비슷해지도록 연습하세요.

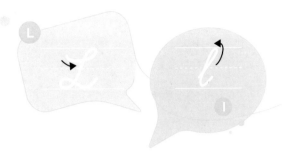

L L L L L L L L

l l l l l l

lie
거짓말(하다)

lie

lie lie lie

long
긴

long

long long long

lunch
점심

lunch

lunch lunch lunch

listen
나이

listen

listen listen listen

23

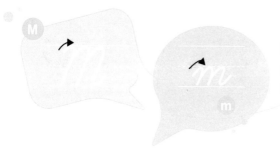

Tip

대문자 M, 소문자 m은 동일하게 두 번 굽어지는 부분의
크기와 폭이 비슷해지도록 연습하세요.

$\mathcal{M}$ $\mathcal{M}$ $\mathcal{M}$ $\mathcal{M}$ $\mathcal{M}$ $\mathcal{M}$

m m m m m m

map
지도

map 　　*map map map*

moon
달

moon 　　*moon moon moon*

model
모형, 표본, 모델

model 　　*model model model*

morning
아침

morning 　　*morning morning morning*

24

필기체 m과 n을 이어 쓸 때는 구분하기 어려울 수 있습니다. *mn* 어떻게 그 차이를 느끼시나요? mn? nm?

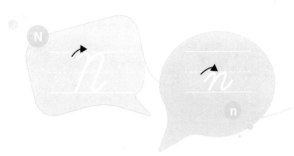

n n n n n n n

n n n n n

new
새로운

new   *new new new*

next
다음의

next   *next next next*

note
노트, 짧은 편지

note   *note note note*

night
밤

night   *night night night*

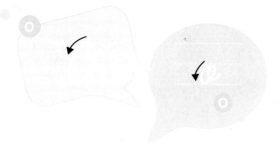

Tip

소문자 o (*o*)와 소문자 e (*e*)가 단어 중간에 나올 때는 구분하기가 어려울 수 있으니 단어 의미로 확인합니다.

O O O O O O O

o o o o o o o

out
밖에

out   *out out out*

old
늙은, 오래된

old   *old old old*

okay
좋아

okay   *okay okay okay*

orange
오렌지

orange   *orange orange orange*

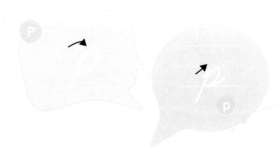

Tip

대문자 P와 소문자 p는 별다른 특징이 없는 듯합니다.
피나게 연습을 해야 할까요? ^^

p p p p p p p

p p p p p p

pen
펜, 볼펜

pen *pen pen pen*

push
밀다

push *push push push*

point
끝, 점

point *point point point*

picture
사진, 그림

picture *picture picture picture*

Tip

소문자 g (*g*)와 소문자 q (*q*)는 그 모양이 비슷하여 혼동하기 쉽습니다. 끝부분을 비교해보세요.

Q Q Q Q Q Q

q q q q q q

quiet
조용한

quiet   *quiet quiet quiet*

quick
빠른

quick   *quick quick quick*

queen
여왕

queen   *queen queen queen*

question
질문

question   *question question question*

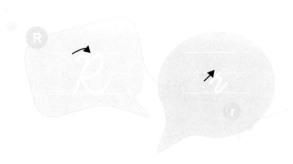

대문자 K (K)를 다른 글자와 빠르게 이어 쓰다 보면
대문자 R (R)처럼 써질때가 있습니다. 주의하세요.

$\mathcal{R}$ $\mathcal{R}$ $\mathcal{R}$ $\mathcal{R}$ $\mathcal{R}$ $\mathcal{R}$ $\mathcal{R}$

r r r r r

red
빨간

red　　*red red red*

rain
비

rain　　*rain rain rain*

ready
준비된

ready　　*ready ready ready*

rocket
로켓

rocket　　*rocket rocket rocket*

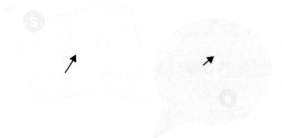

Tip

대문자 G (𝒢)와 S (𝒮), 소문자 s (𝒔)와 r (𝒓)은
그 모양이 비슷하여 혼동하기 쉽습니다.

𝒮 𝒮 𝒮 𝒮 𝒮 𝒮

𝒔 𝒔 𝒔 𝒔 𝒔 𝒔 𝒔

say
말하다

say　　*say say say*

snow
눈

snow　　*snow snow snow*

stamp
짓밟다, 도장 찍다

stamp　　*stamp stamp stamp*

switch
스위치

switch　　*switch switch switch*

Tip

대문자 T (𝒯)와 F (ℱ)는 그 모양이 비슷하여 혼동하기
쉽습니다. 필기체 F의 중간과 아래가 다름을 확인하세요.

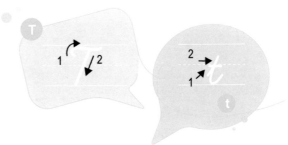

𝒯 𝒯 𝒯 𝒯 𝒯 𝒯

𝓉 𝓉 𝓉 𝓉 𝓉 𝓉

this
이것

this   *this this this*

today
오늘

today   *today today today*

travel
여행하다

travel   *travel travel travel*

through
통과하여

through   *through through through*

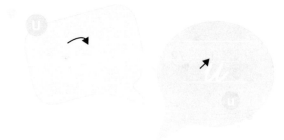

Tip

대문자 U는 처음 시작을 둥글게 말아 내리고, 소문자 u는
굽어 올려서 날카롭게 내려옵니다.

$\mathcal{U}$ $\mathcal{U}$ $\mathcal{U}$ $\mathcal{U}$ $\mathcal{U}$ $\mathcal{U}$

u u u u u u

use
사용하다

use   *use use use*

until
〜까지

until   *until until until*

under
아래에

under   *under under under*

umbrella
우산

umbrella   *umbrella umbrella umbrella*

Tip

대문자 U ($\mathcal{U}$)와 소문자 v ($\mathcal{v}$), 소문자 u ($\mathcal{u}$)와 v ($\mathcal{v}$)는
그 모양이 비슷하여 혼동하기 쉽습니다.

$\mathcal{V}$ $\mathcal{V}$ $\mathcal{V}$ $\mathcal{V}$ $\mathcal{V}$ $\mathcal{V}$

$\mathcal{v}$ $\mathcal{v}$ $\mathcal{v}$ $\mathcal{v}$ $\mathcal{v}$ $\mathcal{v}$ $\mathcal{v}$

very
매우

very　　　*very very very*

video
비디오

video　　　*video video video*

visit
방문하다

visit　　　*visit visit visit*

village
마을

village　　　*village village village*

Tip

알파벳 V를 충분히 연습하셨죠? 알파벳 W는 두 번 굽어 올라가는 부분의 폭을 비슷하게 쓰세요

$\mathcal{W}$ $\mathcal{W}$ $\mathcal{W}$ $\mathcal{W}$ $\mathcal{W}$ $\mathcal{W}$ $\mathcal{W}$ $\mathcal{W}$

w w w w w w w w

why
왜

why　　*why why why*

wear
입다

wear　　*wear wear wear*

wait
기다리다

wait　　*wait wait wait*

wrong
나쁜, 옳지 못한

wrong　　*wrong wrong wrong*

34

알파벳 X는 2획으로 씁니다. 굽어지는 획을 먼저 하고,
사선으로 그려지는 부분을 그다음 순으로 쓰세요.

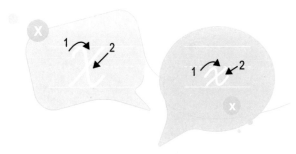

$\mathcal{X}$ $\mathcal{X}$ $\mathcal{X}$ $\mathcal{X}$ $\mathcal{X}$ $\mathcal{X}$ $\mathcal{X}$ $\mathcal{X}$

x x x x x

x-mas
크리스마스

$x\text{-}mas$ $\qquad$ $x\text{-}mas$ $x\text{-}mas$ $x\text{-}mas$

x-ray
엑스레이

$x\text{-}ray$ $\qquad$ $x\text{-}ray$ $x\text{-}ray$ $x\text{-}ray$

xerox
복사(하다)

$xerox$ $\qquad$ $xerox$ $xerox$ $xerox$

xylitol
자일리톨

$xylitol$ $\qquad$ $xylitol$ $xylitol$ $xylitol$

알파벳 V ($\mathcal{U}$ u)와 소문자 g (g) 뒷부분을 합성시켜 놓은 듯 합니다. 자연스럽게 이어 쓰도록 연습하세요.

$\mathcal{Y}$ $\mathcal{Y}$ $\mathcal{Y}$ $\mathcal{Y}$ $\mathcal{Y}$ $\mathcal{Y}$

y y y y y y

you
너, 너희들

you   *you you you*

yes
예, 그렇습니다

yes   *yes yes yes*

year
해, 년

year   *year year year*

yellow
노란색의

yellow   *yellow yellow yellow*

숫자 3자를 먼저 쓰고 그 아래에 소문자 g (*g*) 뒷부분을
생각하며 써보세요. 자연스럽게 이어질 것입니다.

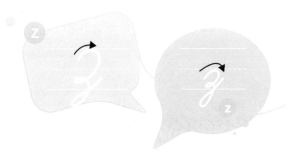

z z z z z z z z

z z z z z z z

zoo
동물원

zoo   *zoo zoo zoo*

zero
숫자 0

zero   *zero zero zero*

zone
지역

zone   *zone zone zone*

zenith
정점, 절정

zenith   *zenith zenith zenith*

지금까지 충분히 연습하셨다면 a~z까지 이어 써볼까요?

홈페이지(www.pub365.co.kr)에서 필기체 연습용 워크시트를 다운받을 수 있습니다.

abcdefghijklmnopqrstuvwxyz

abcdefghijklmnopqrstuvwxyz

abcdefghijklmnopqrstuvwxyz

abcdefghijklmnopqrstuvwxyz

abcdefghijklmnopqrstuvwxyz

abcdefghijklmnopqrstuvwxyz

abcdefghijklmnopqrstuvwxyz

abcdefghijklmnopqrstuvwxyz

Part 2

단어 연습

숫자를 영어 필기체로 써보세요.

one
1

one one one

two
2

two two two

three
3

three three three

four
4

four four four

five
5

five five five

six
6

six six six

seven
7

seven seven seven

eight
8

eight eight eight

nine
9

nine nine nine

ten
10

ten ten ten

eleven
11

eleven eleven eleven

twelve
12

twelve twelve twelve

thirteen
13

thirteen thirteen thirteen

fourteen
14

fourteen fourteen fourteen

fifteen
15

fifteen fifteen fifteen

twenty
20

twenty twenty twenty

thirty
30

thirty thirty thirty

forty
40

forty forty forty

fifty
50

fifty fifty fifty

sixty
60

sixty sixty sixty

seventy
70

seventy seventy seventy

eighty
80

eighty eighty eighty

ninety
90

ninety ninety ninety

hundred
100

hundred hundred hundred

달력의 월을 영어 필기체로 써보세요.

January
1월

January January January

February
2월

February February February

March
3월

March March March

April
4월

April April April

May
5월

May May May

June
6월

June June June

July
7월

July July July

August
8월

August August August

September
9월

September September September

October
10월

October October October

November
11월

November November November

December
12월

December December December

달력의 요일을 영어 필기체로 써보세요.

Monday
월요일

Monday Monday Monday

Tuesday
화요일

Tuesday Tuesday Tuesday

Wednesday
수요일

Wednesday Wednesday Wednesday

Thursday
목요일

Thursday Thursday Thursday

Friday
금요일

Friday Friday Friday

Saturday
토요일

Saturday Saturday Saturday

Sunday
일요일

Sunday Sunday Sunday

Week
주

Week Week Week

Month
월

Month Month Month

Year
년

Year Year Year

자신의 생년월일, 요일을 영어 필기체로 써보세요.

다양한 색깔을 영어 필기체로 써보세요.

red
빨간색

red red red

orange
주황색

orange orange orange

pink
분홍색

pink pink pink

yellow
노란색

yellow yellow yellow

green
초록색

green green green

blue
파란색

blue blue blue

sky blue
하늘색

sky blue sky blue sky blue

dark blue
남색

dark blue dark blue dark blue

brown
갈색

brown brown brown

violet
보라색

violet violet violet

black
검은색

black black black

white
흰색

white white white

우리나라 성씨를 영어 필기체로 써보세요.

Kim
김

Kim Kim Kim

Lee
이

Lee Lee Lee

Park
박

Park Park Park

Choi
최

Choi Choi Choi

Jung
정

Jung Jung Jung

Kang
강

Kang Kang Kang

Cho
조

Cho Cho Cho

Yoon
윤

Yoon Yoon Yoon

Jang
장

Jang Jang Jang

Lim
임

Lim Lim Lim

Han
한

Han Han Han

Shin
신

Shin Shin Shin

우리나라 성씨를 영어 필기체로 써보세요.

Oh
오

Oh Oh Oh

Seo
서

Seo Seo Seo

Kwon
권

Kwon Kwon Kwon

Hwang
황

Hwang Hwang Hwang

Song
송

Song Song Song

Ahn
안

Ahn Ahn Ahn

Yoo
유

Yoo Yoo Yoo

Hong
홍

Hong Hong Hong

Jeon
전

Jeon Jeon Jeon

Ko
고

Ko Ko Ko

Moon
문

Moon Moon Moon

Son
손

Son Son Son

남자 이름을 영어 필기체로 써보세요.

Bo Geom
보검

Bo Geom Bo Geom Bo Geom

Jun Yeol
준열

Jun Yeol Jun Yeol Jun Yeol

Joong Ki
중기

Joong Ki Joong Ki Joong Ki

Jong Seok
종석

Jong Seok Jong Seok Jong Seok

Ho Jun
호준

Ho Jun Ho Jun Ho Jun

Rae Won
래원

Rae Won Rae Won Rae Won

John
존

John John John

Andrew
앤드류

Andrew Andrew Andrew

Michael
마이클

Michael Michael Michael

Eric
에릭

Eric Eric Eric

David
데이비드

David David David

Henry
헨리

Henry Henry Henry

여자 이름을 영어 필기체로 써보세요.

Go Eun
고은

Go Eun Go Eun Go Eun

Ye Won
예원

Ye Won Ye Won Ye Won

Hyo Ju
효주

Hyo Ju Hyo Ju Hyo Ju

Ji Yeon
지연

Ji Yeon Ji Yeon Ji Yeon

Yu Jung
유정

Yu Jung Yu Jung Yu Jung

Shin Hye
신혜

Shin Hye Shin Hye Shin Hye

Chloe
클로이

Chloe Chloe Chloe

Lisa
리사

Lisa Lisa Lisa

Rachel
레이첼

Rachel Rachel Rachel

Victoria
빅토리아

Victoria Victoria Victoria

Eva
에바

Eva Eva Eva

Sarah
사라

Sarah Sarah Sarah

나라 이름을 영어 필기체로 써보세요.

Korea
한국

Korea Korea Korea

China
중국

China China China

Japan
일본

Japan Japan Japan

Thailand
태국

Thailand Thailand Thailand

Vietnam
베트남

Vietnam Vietnam Vietnam

Singapore
싱가포르

Singapore Singapore Singapore

Australia
호주

Australia Australia Australia

Norway
노르웨이

Norway Norway Norway

Kenya
케냐

Kenya Kenya Kenya

England
잉글랜드

England England England

Denmark
덴마크

Denmark Denmark Denmark

Sweden
스웨덴

Sweden Sweden Sweden

나라 이름을 영어 필기체로 써보세요.

Belgium
벨기에   *Belgium Belgium Belgium*

France
프랑스   *France France France*

Germany
독일   *Germany Germany Germany*

Netherlands
네덜란드   *Netherlands Netherlands Netherlands*

Greece
그리스   *Greece Greece Greece*

Italy
이탈리아   *Italy Italy Italy*

Portugal
포르투갈

Portugal Portugal Portugal

Spain
스페인

Spain Spain Spain

Russia
러시아

Russia Russia Russia

Canada
캐나다

Canada Canada Canada

Mexico
멕시코

Mexico Mexico Mexico

Brazil
브라질

Brazil Brazil Brazil

기념일을 영어 필기체로 써보세요.

New Years Day
새해

New Years Day New Years Day

Valentine's Day
밸런타인데이

Valentine's Day Valentine's Day

Labor Day
노동절

Labor Day Labor Day

Mother's Day
어머니의 날

Mother's Day Mother's Day

Father's Day
아버지의 날

Father's Day Father's Day

Memorial Day
현충일

Memorial Day Memorial Day

Halloween
핼러윈

Halloween Halloween

Christmas
크리스마스

Christmas Christmas

Easter
부활절

Easter Easter

Birthday
생일

Birthday Birthday

Fool's Day
만우절

Fool's Day Fool's Day

anniversary
기념일

anniversary anniversary

Part 3

패턴 연습

자주 사용되는 접두어를 영어 필기체로 써보세요.

Before, Forward (앞, 전진)의 뜻이 있는 것 : pre-, pro-

predict 예언하다 / **pre**vious 앞의

predict predict predict

previous previous previous

proceed 진행하다 / **pro**gress 진보하다

proceed proceed proceed

progress progress progress

After, Backward (뒤, 후퇴)의 뜻이 있는 것 : post-

posterity 자손 / **post**pone 연기하다

posterity posterity posterity

postpone postpone postpone

Down, Under (아래)의 뜻이 있는 것 : sub-, sup-

submarine 잠수함 / **sub**way 지하철

submarine submarine submarine

subway subway subway

support 지탱하다 / **sup**pose 예상하다

support support support

suppose suppose suppose

Negative (부정)의 뜻이 있는 것 : mis-, dis-

misfortune 불행 / **mis**fit 부적합

misfortune misfortune misfortune

misfit misfit misfit

discomfort 불쾌 / **dis**honest 정직하지 않은

discomfort discomfort discomfort

dishonest dishonest dishonest

Against (반대)의 뜻이 있는 것 : anti-

antidote 해독제 / **anti**pathy 반감

antidote antidote antidote

antipathy antipathy antipathy

Away, From (분리)의 뜻이 있는 것 : de-, se-

decline 거절하다 / **de**liver 배달하다

decline decline decline

deliver deliver deliver

separate 분리하다 / **se**rve 절단하다

separate separate separate

serve serve serve

65

자주 사용되는 접두어를 영어 필기체로 써보세요.

In, Within (가운데, 안)의 뜻이 있는 것 : en-, inter-

enjoy 즐기다 / **en**velope 봉투

enjoy enjoy enjoy

envelope envelope envelope

international 국제의 / **inter**cept 도중에서 빼앗다

international international international

intercept intercept intercept

After, Backward (뒤, 후퇴)의 뜻이 있는 것 : ex-

exhibit 전시하다 / **ex**pose 노출하다

exhibit exhibit exhibit

expose expose expose

With (합동)의 뜻이 있는 것 : com-, sym-

compassion 동정 / **com**panion 동료, 상대

compassion compassion compassion

companion companion companion

sympathy 동정심 / **sym**phony 교향곡

sympathy sympathy sympathy

symphony symphony symphony

수에 관한 것 : uni-, twi-

uniform 제복 / **uni**t 단위

uniform uniform uniform

unit unit unit

twice 두 번 / **twi**n 쌍둥이

twice twice twice

twin twin twin

Around (주위)의 뜻이 있는 것 : circu-

circuit 주변 / **circu**late 순환하다

circuit circuit circuit

circulate circulate circulate

Good (좋음)의 뜻이 있는 것 : beni-, wel-

benign 친절한 / **beni**son 축복

benign benign benign

benison benison benison

welcome 환영하다 / **wel**fare 행복

welcome welcome welcome

welfare welfare welfare

자주 사용되는 접미어를 영어 필기체로 써보세요.

Abstract Noun (추상명사)을 만드는 것 : -al, -ure

survival 살아남음 / denial 부정

survival survival survival

denial denial denial

culture 문화 / adventure 모험

culture culture culture

adventure adventure adventure

Major (전공)의 뜻이 있는 것 : -ics

mathematics 수학 / physics 물리학

mathematics mathematics mathematics

physics physics physics

Plenty (충분한)의 뜻이 있는 것 : -ful, -ous

careful 주의 깊은 / useful 유용한

careful careful careful

useful useful useful

famous 유명한 / perilous 위태로운

famous famous famous

perilous perilous perilous

Ability (가능성)의 뜻이 있는 것 : –able, –ible

eat**able** 먹을 수 있는 / lov**able** 사랑스러운

eatable eatable eatable

lovable lovable lovable

cred**ible** 믿을 수 있는 / impress**ible** 느끼기 쉬운

impressible impressible impressible

credible credible credible

Like (~와 같은,~다운)의 뜻이 있는 것 : –like

man**like** 남자다운 / god**like** 신과 같은

manlike manlike manlike

godlike godlike godlike

Direction (방향)의 뜻이 있는 것 : –ern, –wards

west**ern** 서쪽의 / east**ern** 동쪽의

western western western

eastern eastern eastern

down**wards** 아래쪽으로 / for**wards** 전방에

downwards downwards downwards

forwards forwards forwards

자주 사용되는 평서형 패턴을 영어 필기체로 써보세요.

Let's ··· / ~하자

Let's go shopping. 쇼핑하러 가자.

Let's go shopping.

Let's eat out. 외식하자.

Let's eat out.

I need ··· / ~가 필요해

I need your help. 네 도움이 필요해.

I need your help.

I need a rest. 휴식이 필요해.

I need a rest.

It seems like ··· / ~인 것 같아

It seems like yesterday. 마치 어제인 것 같아.

It seems like yesterday.

It seems like I'm dreaming. 꿈을 꾸고 있는 것 같아.

It seems like I'm dreaming.

I don't think ⋯ / ~것 같지 않아

I don't think so. 그런 것 같지 않아.

I don't think so.

I don't think I can do that. 내가 할 수 있을 것 같지 않아.

I don't think I can do that.

There is ⋯ / ~가 있어

There is a better way. 더 좋은 방법이 있어.

There is a better way.

There is a good example. 좋은 예가 있어.

There is a good example.

I spent ⋯ / ~에 (시간/돈) 썼어

I spent all my money. 내 돈을 모두 다 썼어.

I spent all my money.

I spent five days. 5일이나 투자했어.

I spent five days.

자주 사용되는 평서형 패턴을 영어 필기체로 써보세요.

It depends on … / ~따라 달라

It depends on you. 너에 따라 달라.

It depends on you.

It depends on your taste. 취향에 따라 달라.

It depends on your taste.

I have no … / 나는 ~이(가) 없어

I have no umbrella. 나는 우산이 없어.

I have no umbrella.

I have no boyfriend. 나는 남자 친구가 없어.

I have no boyfriend.

I forgot to … / ~하는 걸 잊었어

I forgot to finish my homework. 숙제하는 것을 잊었어.

I forgot to finish my homework.

I forgot to leave the message. 메시지를 남기는 걸 잊었어.

I forgot to leave the message.

I don't care ··· / ~ 해도 상관없어

I don't care how much it costs. 얼마든 상관없어.

I don't care how much it costs.

I don't care what people say. 사람들이 뭐라고 하든 상관없어.

I don't care what people say.

You should ··· / ~하는 게 좋을 거야

You should study English. 영어 공부를 하는 게 좋을 거야.

You should study English.

You should have a dream. 꿈을 갖는 게 좋을 거야.

You should have a dream.

It's worth ··· / ~할 만해

It's worth visiting. 방문할 만해.

It's worth visiting.

It's worth investing. 투자할 만해.

It's worth investing.

자주 사용되는 의문형 패턴을 영어 필기체로 써보세요.

How can I ···? / 어떻게 ~하나요?

How can I get there? 거기 어떻게 가나요?

How can I get there?

How can I forget? 어떻게 잊나요?

How can I forget?

Is there any ···? / ~이(가) 있나요?

Is there any reason? 이유가 있나요?

Is there any reason?

Is there any way to find out? 찾을 방법이 있나요?

Is there any way to find out?

May I see ···? / 제가 ~을 볼 수 있을까요?

May I see your ticket? 티켓을 볼 수 있을까요?

May I see your ticket?

May I see your driver's license? 면허증을 볼 수 있을까요?

May I see your driver's license?

How much is …? ~얼마에요?

How much is it? 그거 얼마에요?

How much is it?

How much is this purse? 이 지갑은 얼마에요?

How much is this purse?

Do you mind …? / ~해도 괜찮을까요?

Do you mind opening the window? 창문 좀 열어도 될까요?

Do you mind opening the window?

Do you mind if I ask you a question? 질문해도 괜찮을까요?

Do you mind if I ask you a question?

When did you …? / 언제 ~했나요?

When did you start? 언제 시작했어?

When did you start?

When did you call him? 언제 그에게 전화했어?

When did you call him?

자주 사용되는 의문형 패턴을 영어 필기체로 써보세요.

How about ...? / ~은 어때요?

How about this weekend? 이번 주는 어때?

How about this weekend?

How about dinner tonight? 오늘 저녁 먹는 거 어때?

How about dinner tonight?

Who is your ...? / 누가 당신의 ~인가요?

Who is your boss? 너희 대표는 누구야?

Who is your boss?

Who is your favorite singer? 가장 좋아하는 가수는 누구인가요?

Who is your favorite singer?

Do you want ...? / 당신은 ~을 원하나요?

Do you want some water? 물 좀 드릴까요?

Do you want some water?

Do you want to know? 알고 싶나요?

Do you want to know?

홈페이지(www.pub365.co.kr)에서 필기체 연습용 워크시트를 다운받을 수 있습니다.

What happened to ⋯? / ~에게 무슨 일이야?

What happened to you? 너 무슨 일이야?

What happened to you?

What happened to your car? 당신 차 왜 그래요?

What happened to your car?

What is your ⋯? / 당신의 ~는 뭔가요?

What is your problem? 당신의 문제가 뭔가요?

What is your problem?

What is your favorite sport? 당신이 가장 좋아하는 스포츠는 뭔가요?

What is your favorite sport?

Where can I ⋯? / 어디로 ~하면 되나요?

Where can I apply? 어디로 신청하면 되나요?

Where can I apply?

Where can I contact them? 어디로 연락하면 되나요?

Where can I contact them?

Part 4

문장 연습

인생의 지침이 되는 명언을 영어 필기체로 써보세요.

Raise your head! 고개를 들어라!

Raise your head!

Think different! 다르게 생각해보라!

Think different!

Who dares, wins. 도전하는 자가, 승리한다.

Who dares, wins.

No pain, no gain. 고통 없이는 얻는 것도 없다.

No pain, no gain.

Easy come easy go. 쉽게 온 것은 쉽게 간다.

Easy come easy go.

Boys, be ambitious! 소년이여, 야망을 품어라!

Boys, be ambitious!

Try hard, Try hard! 노력하고, 또 노력하라!

Try hard, Try hard!

No sweat, no sweet. 땀 없이는, 달콤함도 없다.

No sweat, no sweet.

Time is life itself. 시간은 삶 그 차체이다.

Time is life itself.

There is no Destiny. 운명이란 없다.

There is no Destiny.

인생의 지침이 되는 명언을 영어 필기체로 써보세요.

Look before you leap. 도약하기 전에 먼저 살펴보라.

Look before you leap.

Don't worry be happy. 걱정마, 다 잘 될 거야.

Don't worry be happy.

The life is only once. 인생은 오직 한 번뿐이다.

The life is only once.

Shout out "Once more!" 큰 소리로 외쳐라 – "한 번 더"를!

Shout out "Once more!"

Be friends with fears. 공포심과 친구가 되어라.

Be friends with fears.

Practice makes perfect. 연습이 최고를 만든다.

Practice makes perfect.

Better late than never. 아예 안 하는 것보다는 늦게라도 하는 게 낫다.

Better late than never.

Pardon all but yourself. 모든 사람을 용서하라. 너 자신은 제외하고!

Pardon all but yourself.

Every path has its puddle. 모든 길에는 웅덩이가 있는 법.

Every path has its puddle.

Big goals get big results. 큰 목표가 큰 결과를 가져온다.

Big goals get big results.

인생의 지침이 되는 명언을 영어 필기체로 써보세요.

Nothing seek, nothing find. 구하지 않으면, 얻는 것도 없다.

Nothing seek, nothing find.

Rome is not built in a day. 로마는 하룻밤에 만들어지는 게 아니다.

Rome is not built in a day.

I must do what I want to do. 나는 한다면 하는 놈이야.

I must do what I want to do.

Early birds catch the worms. 일찍 일어나는 새가 벌레를 잡는다.

Early birds catch the worms.

Slow and steady win the race. 천천히 그리고 꾸준히 하면 이긴다.

Slow and steady win the race.

Never, never, never, give up. 절대로, 절대로 포기하지 마라.

Never, never, never, give up.

A sound mind in a sound body. 건강한 몸에 건강한 정신이 깃든다.

A sound mind in a sound body.

Make hay while the sun shines. 해가 비추는 동안에 건초를 말려라.

Make hay while the sun shines.

As ones sows so shall he reap. 뿌린 만큼 거둔다.

As ones sows so shall he reap.

One is never too old to learn. 배움에는 나이가 없다.

One is never too old to learn.

인생의 지침이 되는 명언을 영어 필기체로 써보세요.

Faith without deeds is useless. 실행이 없는 믿음은 쓸모가 없다.

Faith without deeds is useless.

A Bold Attempt is half Success. 과감한 시도는 절반은 성공한 것이다.

A Bold Attempt is half Success.

Success doesn't come overnight. 성공은 하룻밤 사이에 오지 않는다.

Success doesn't come overnight.

Everything is gonna be alright! 모든 것은 잘 되어갈 거야!

Everything is gonna be alright!

Opportunity seldom knocks twice. 기회는 좀처럼 두 번 오지 않는다.

Opportunity seldom knocks twice.

The real effort never betrays me. 진정한 노력은 결코 나를 배신하지 않는다!

The real effort never betrays me.

Think of the end before you begin. 시작하기 전에 끝을 생각하라.

Think of the end before you begin.

You can't have what you don't want. 네가 원하지 않은 것은 가질 수 없다.

You can't have what you don't want.

Without a goal, you cannot survive. 목표 없이는 살아남을 수 없다.

Without a goal, you cannot survive.

Everything comes to those who wait. 모든 것은 기다리는 자에게 온다.

Everything comes to those who wait.

인생의 지침이 되는 명언을 영어 필기체로 써보세요.

Diligence is the mother of good luck. 근면함은 행운의 어머니이다.

Diligence is the mother of good luck.

Try your best rather than be the best. 최고가 되기보다는, 최선을 다하자.

Try your best rather than be the best.

Ability is decided by one's own effort. 능력은 자신의 노력으로 결정된다.

Ability is decided by one's own effort.

Faithfulness makes all things possible. 성실함은 모든 것을 가능케 한다.

Faithfulness makes all things possible.

We will either find a way, or make one. 우리는 둘 중 하나 – 길을 찾거나, 만들거나!

We will either find a way, or make one.

Everything will be done if you try hard. 열심히 노력한다면, 모든 것은 성취될 것이다.

Everything will be done if you try hard.

I'm a slow walker, but I never walk back. 나는 느리게 가는 사람이지만, 결코 뒤로 가지는 않습니다.

I'm a slow walker, but I never walk back.

Build a dream and the dream will build you. 꿈을 구축하면, 꿈이 너를 만들 것이다.

Build a dream and the dream will build you.

Luck is when preparedness meets opportunity. 운이란 준비가 기회를 만나는 때이다.

Luck is when preparedness meets opportunity.

The word 'impossible' is not in my dictionary. 내 사전에 불가능이란 없다.

The word 'impossible' is not in my dictionary.

왼쪽 페이지의 긴 문장을 보고 우측에 영어 필기체로 써보세요.

Dear Aunt Beatrice

Thank you so much for the great time we had on your farm this past summer. I was very impressed by the way you and Uncle Bill have set up your farm. The time spent with the cows and the pigs was not only fun but I learned a lot about how to care for these animals. I also enjoyed the horses which you have on the farm. My favorite was Comet he was so gentle and allowed me to ride him around the pen. I also had a super time with your dogs, Rex and Regina; they were awesome dogs and played with me for the entire day sometime. I also have to mention the delicious home cooked meals you made for Uncle Bill and me. We always had fresh vegetables from your garden and fresh milk from Daisy and Margaret, your milking cows. Thank you for an unforgettable summer in which I learned many things which I plan on sharing with my new classmates.

친애하는 Beatrice 이모님께

　지난여름 저희에게 농장에서 좋은 시간을 보내게 해주셔서 정말 감사드립니다. 이모님과 Bill 삼촌께서 만들어 놓으신 농장에 깊은 감명을 받았습니다. 소와 돼지들과 함께 보낸 시간은 즐거웠을 뿐만 아니라 이러한 동물들을 어떻게 돌보는지에 대해서도 많이 배울 수 있었던 시간이었습니다. 또한 농장의 말과도 좋은 시간을 보냈습니다. 제가 가장 좋아했던 Comet은 아주 유순했고 우리 근처에서 탈 수도 있게 해 주었습니다. Rex와 Regina랑도 매우 재미있는 시간을 보냈는데 그들은 정말 멋지고 어느 날은 저와 하루 종일 놀기도 하였습니다. 이모님과 삼촌께서 만들어 주신 맛있는 음식도 얘기하지 않을 수가 없습니다. 저희는 항상 정원에 있는 신선한 야채를 먹었고 이모님의 젖소인 Daisy와 Margaret으로부터 신선한 우유를 마셨습니다. 새로운 친구들과 나눌 수 있도록 많은 것을 배울 수 있었던 잊을 수 없는 여름을 보내게 해주셔서 감사드립니다.

Dear Aunt Beatrice

Thank you so much for the great time we had on your farm this past summer. I was very impressed by the way you and Uncle Bill have set up your farm. The time spent with the cows and the pigs was not only fun but I learned a lot about how to care for these animals. I also enjoyed the horses which you have on the farm. My favorite was Comet he was so gentle and allowed me to ride him around the pen. I also had a super time with your dogs, Rex and Regina, they were awesome dogs and played with me for the entire day sometime. I also have to mention the delicious home cooked meals you made for Uncle Bill and me. We always had fresh vegetables from your garden and fresh milk from Daisy and Margaret, your milking cows. Thank you for an unforgettable summer in which I learned many things which I plan on sharing with my new classmates.

왼쪽 페이지의 긴 문장을 보고 우측에 영어 필기체로 써보세요.

Dear Harry,

I would like you to be the main speaker at this month's meeting. The topic of the talk will be how can we make our stores better? I would ask that you think of five things to improve our stores (appearance, customer service, promotions etc.) This will hopefully lead to an open discussion by the other managers. I look forward to your presentation and hope that it inspires the other managers to go the extra mile in improving our stores. Please call if you have any questions or concerns about the upcoming meeting. I would also ask you to supply me with a copy of your talk so I may review it prior to the presentation. I would like to have it by next Friday if that is convenient for you.

Harry씨께,

　Harry씨께서 이번 달 회의의 주 발표자가 되어주셨으면 좋겠습니다. 발표의 주제는 어떻게 하면 가게를 더 좋게 만들지에 대한 것입니다. Harry씨께서 가게 개선을 위해 5가지 것들(외관, 고객 서비스, 판촉 상품 등)을 생각해 오시기 바랍니다. 이것들이 다른 매니저들과의 토론으로 이어질 수 있으면 좋겠습니다. Harry씨의 발표를 기대하고 있고 발표가 가게의 발전으로 이어질 수 있도록 매니저들의 사기를 돋울 수 있는 계기가 되기를 바랍니다. 질문이 있으시거나 다가오는 회의에 대한 안건이 있으시면 전화 주시기 바랍니다. 또한 발표에 앞서 제가 검토할 수 있도록 발표 복사본을 보내주셨으면 좋겠습니다. 괜찮으시다면 다음 주 금요일까지 보내주십시오.

Dear Harry,

I would like you to be the main speaker at this month's meeting. The topic of the talk will be how can we make our stores better? I would ask that you think of five things to improve our stores (appearance, customer service, promotions etc.) This will hopefully lead to an open discussion by the other managers. I look forward to your presentation and hope that it inspires the other managers to go the extra mile in improving our stores. Please call if you have any questions or concerns about the upcoming meeting. I would also ask you to supply me with a copy of your talk so I may review it prior to the presentation. I would like to have it by next Friday if that is convenient for you.

Dear Dr. Bettancourt,

It was great to have spent a couple of hours at the convention getting to know you and your research project better. As I explained then, our company, Major Medical Corporation Inc. is looking to invest in many research projects like your own. What I would require from you is a summary of your project and any test materials you could supply. In return Major Medical would be able to fund your project as a co-partner. Please e-mail the requested documents as soon as possible and I will begin processing a grant application. I look forward to working with you on your very exciting research project. I am attaching some information concerning Major Medical grants in your field of interest.

Bettencourt 박사님께,

　총회에서 박사님을 더 잘 알고 박사님의 연구 프로젝트를 더 잘 알 수 있었던 시간은 정말 즐거웠습니다. 제가 설명해 드린 대로 저희 의료법인 Major는 박사님의 것과 같은 연구 프로젝트의 투자를 찾고 있습니다. 박사님께 부탁드리는 것은 프로젝트의 요약본과 공급 가능한 테스트 자료들입니다. 회답으로 저희는 합작으로 박사님의 연구를 지원할 수 있게 될 것입니다. 제가 부탁드린 자료를 최대한 빨리 이메일로 보내주시면 지원을 받는 것을 추진하겠습니다. 박사님과 함께 흥미로운 연구 프로젝트를 진행하는 것을 기대합니다. Major 의료법인 증서에 관련한 정보를 담은 자료를 첨부하겠습니다.

Dear Dr. Bettancourt,

It was great to have spent a couple of hours at the convention getting to know you and your research project better. As I explained then, our company, Major Medical Corporation, Inc. is looking to invest in many research projects like your own. What I would require from you is a summary of your project and any text materials you could supply. In return Major Medical would be able to fund your project as a co-partner. Please e-mail the requested documents as soon as possible and I will begin processing a grant application. I look forward to working with you on your very exciting research project. I am attaching some information concerning Major Medical grants in your field of interest.

왼쪽 페이지의 긴 문장을 보고 우측에 영어 필기체로 써보세요.

EMERGENCY PARKING

Parking regulations in the event of a significant snowfall The Bedford County Public Works Department would like to inform all Bedford County residents of the emergency parking regulations in the event of a snow or ice storm. If a snow emergency is declared the following parking restrictions are put into effect. All odd numbered sides of the street will be no parking zones from the hours of 7:00 A.M. to 7:00 P.M. There will be no overnight parking on either side of the street. In addition there will be no even side street parking from 7:00 P.M. until 7:00 A.M. the following day. These parking bans will be in effect until the snow emergency is discontinued.

ALL VEHICLES IN VIOLATION OF THESE PAKRKING REGULATIONS WILL BE SUBJECT TO TOWING AND FINES

비상주차

대설로 인한 주차 규제 Bedford주 공익 근로 부서는 모든 Bedford의 거주자들에게 눈과 우빙성 폭풍우로 인한 비상 주차 제한을 알립니다. 눈으로 인한 비상사태가 선포되면 다음과 같은 주차 제한은 효력을 발휘하게 됩니다. 도로의 홀수로 매겨진 쪽은 오전 7시부터 저녁 7시까지 주차 금지 지역이 됩니다. 또한 도로의 어떤 쪽에도 하루를 넘기는 주차는 허용되지 않습니다. 게다가 다음 날 저녁 7시부터 오전 7시까지는 짝수 쪽의 주차가 금지됩니다. 이러한 주차 금지는 눈으로 인한 비상사태가 해지될 때까지 유효합니다.

주차제한을 위반하는 모든 차량은 견인되거나 벌금이 부과될 것임

96

홈페이지(www.pub365.co.kr)에서 필기체 연습용 워크시트를 다운받을 수 있습니다.

Last Friday was September 18th. It was the best day of my life. September 18th is my birthday. I was born in 1994. I am 12 years old now. I am just finishing the 5th grade. When I got up on Friday morning I was so excited. The weather was fine. The sky was clear and the temperature was crisp. But more importantly I am now a preteen. Next year I will be a teenager. I got up and got ready for school. My mom made me my favorite breakfast. She cooked French toast, sausages, and scrambled eggs. After I ate breakfast I went off to school. When I got to school I met my friends. They all wished me a happy birthday. In English class Mrs.Perkins bought me a birthday cake. She always throws a birthday party when it is your birthday. Everyone in the class sang happy birthday to me. Then I blew out the candles. The cake was so delicious. It was an ice cream cake. After school finished I went home. My parents planned to take me out for dinner. I was allowed to go wherever I wanted. I chose Dominoes. I love pizza. Wee ordered a large combination pizza and a large vegetable pizza. We ate like pigs. After dinner we went home. In the car my parents told me they had a surprise for me. When we got home I race into the house. On the table in the living room was a large box. I tore it open. It was a brand new computer. I had wanted a new computer for more than a year. I was so happy.

홈페이지(www.pub365.co.kr)에서 필기체 연습용 워크시트를 다운받을 수 있습니다.

수고하셨습니다. 나만의 멋진 영어 필기체 한번 볼까요?

아래 문장을 써보세요.

The real effort never betrays me!

The real effort never betrays me!
진정한 노력은 결코 나를 배신하지 않는다!

❶

❷

❸